FIRST HERO IN OUTER SPACE

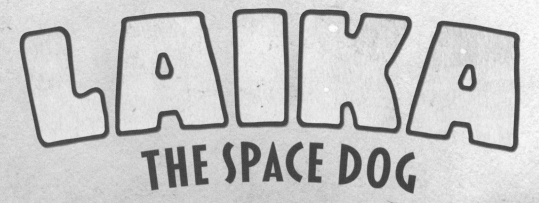

LAIKA
THE SPACE DOG

by JENI WITTROCK   illustrated by SHANNON TOTH

content consultant: Dr. Dave Williams, planetary scientist, National Space Science Data Center, NASA

PICTURE WINDOW BOOKS
a capstone imprint

Through the streets, alleyways, and markets of Moscow,
a small, curly-tailed stray trotted warily. Every day, little
Laika (LIKE-uh) rummaged for food and refuge for the night.

It was late summer, 1956. The Soviet Union prepared to launch *Sputnik*, the world's first satellite, into orbit. But street dogs like Laika knew nothing of outer space. What Laika wanted was food!

When a quiet man approached her, the little dog eyed him carefully. He held out a morsel of food in one hand. But what was in the other hand? Was this a friend?

Laika crept toward the treat—she could almost reach the meat! Then, *whoosh!* went the dogcatcher's net. Laika yipped! She struggled to get free, but it was no use. She was caught.

6

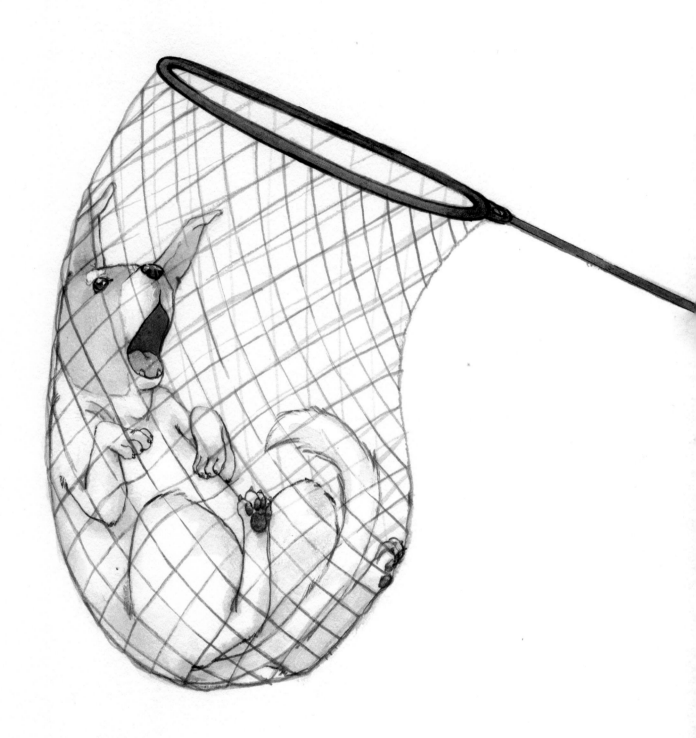

In a rumbling truck, the dogcatcher brought
Laika to the Institute of Aviation Medicine. This laboratory
housed street dogs to be used in scientific tests and missions.

While lab dogs were given food and shelter, they lost all freedom.
A hard road lay ahead for Laika.

Life as a lab dog was difficult. Machines tested how Laika handled extreme speed, pressure, vibration, and noise. Sometimes she was held in a tiny cage for days at a time. She learned to live in a very small space.

Dr. Oleg Gazenko and the trainers at the Institute liked Laika. She stayed calm and always did what they asked. The trainers called her *Kudryavka*, which is Russian for "Little Curly." She was nicknamed *Limonchik*, "Little Lemon," and *Zhuchka*, "Little Bug."

Soon Laika became one of three dogs considered for a special new mission. A second Soviet satellite, *Sputnik 2*, would be launched in less than a month. And this time, there would be a dog on board.

While Laika was finishing her training, *Sputnik 2* was quickly being built. No person or animal had orbited in outer space yet, and scientists were unsure if it was safe. Smaller rockets had flown dogs, mice, monkeys, and rabbits to high altitudes. But none had left Earth's atmosphere.

Laika saw other dogs leave for rocket test flights. Some of them never came back.

Scientists wanted to learn how space travel would affect an animal's body. A special space suit was made just for Laika. It would help her body adjust to changes in pressure. Machines would record Laika's heartbeat, blood pressure, and movements.

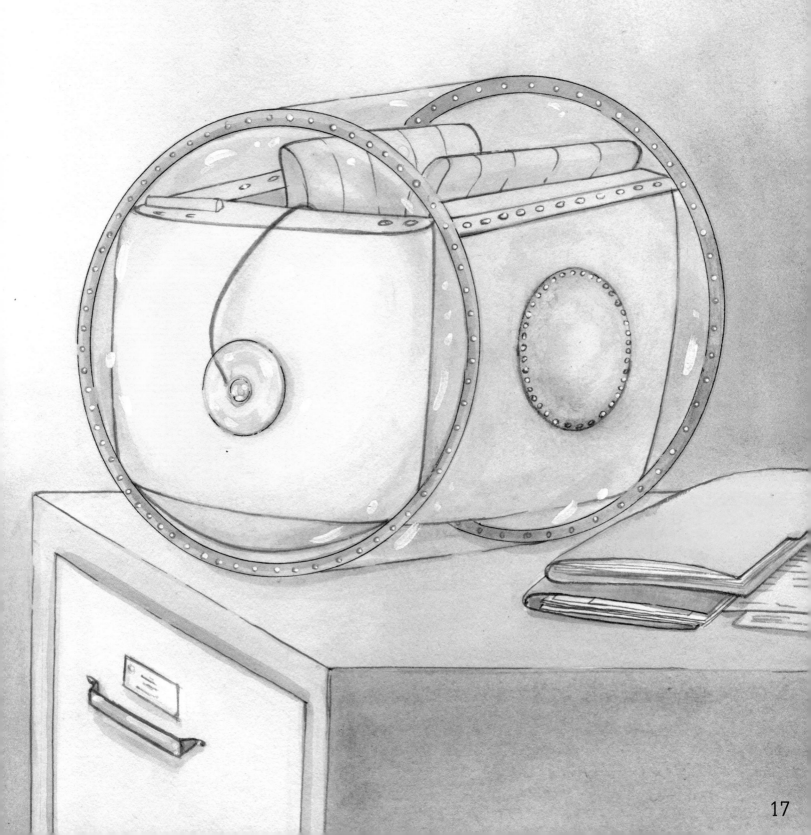

In late October, *Sputnik 2* was almost ready. A small cabin would be attached below the new satellite. It was just big enough for a small dog to sit, stand, and move around a little. A machine was added to dispense food.

On October 25, 1957, a radio report informed the world of Laika's daring mission. Laika had been chosen to travel to outer space in *Sputnik 2*. Soviet audiences listened as Laika barked into the microphone.

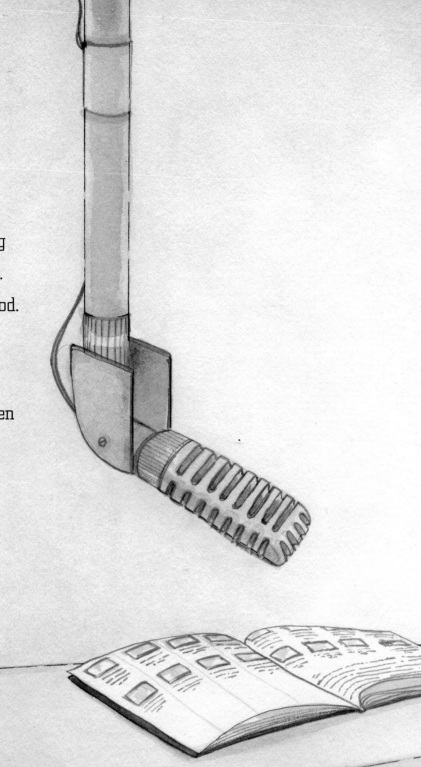

On October 31, 1957, Dr. Gazenko and the trainers suited up Laika one last time. Her handlers said a teary goodbye and wished their Little Curly the best of luck. Strapped inside her tiny cabin, Laika watched them walk away.

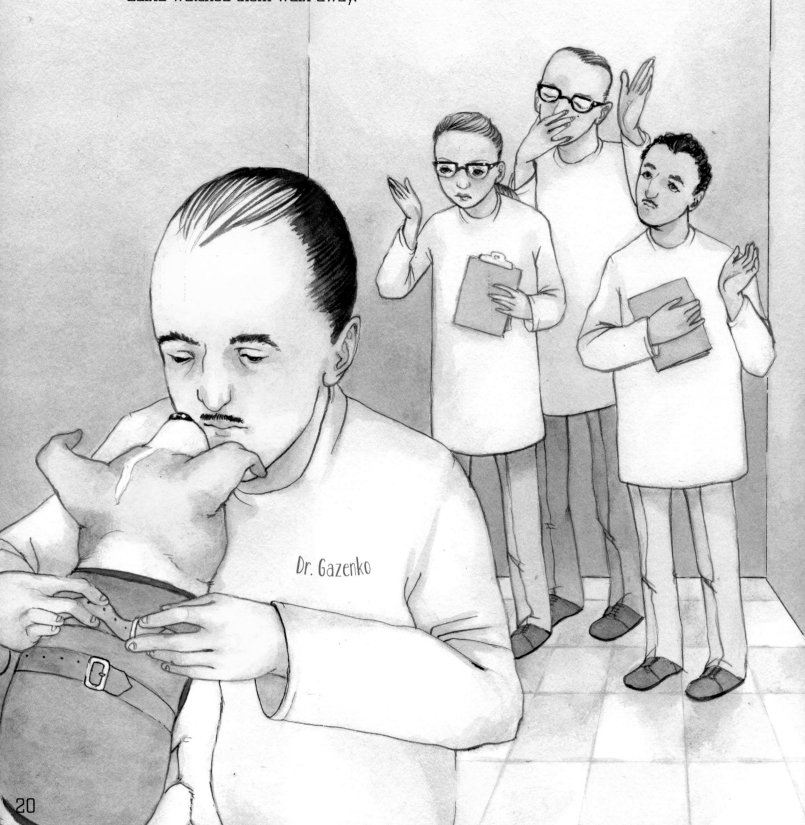

Dr. Gazenko

Laika waited alone in her little cabin. Finally she was transported to the launchpad and prepared for liftoff. Nearly four days passed before *Sputnik 2* was set to launch.

On November 3, 1957, the rocket's engines roared to life. The noise became loud, louder, then deafening. In a fiery blast, *Sputnik 2* lifted off the launchpad. Laika's heart pounded, and she barked in fear. The noise was almost unbearable. Even her training had not been like this. But there was no turning back.

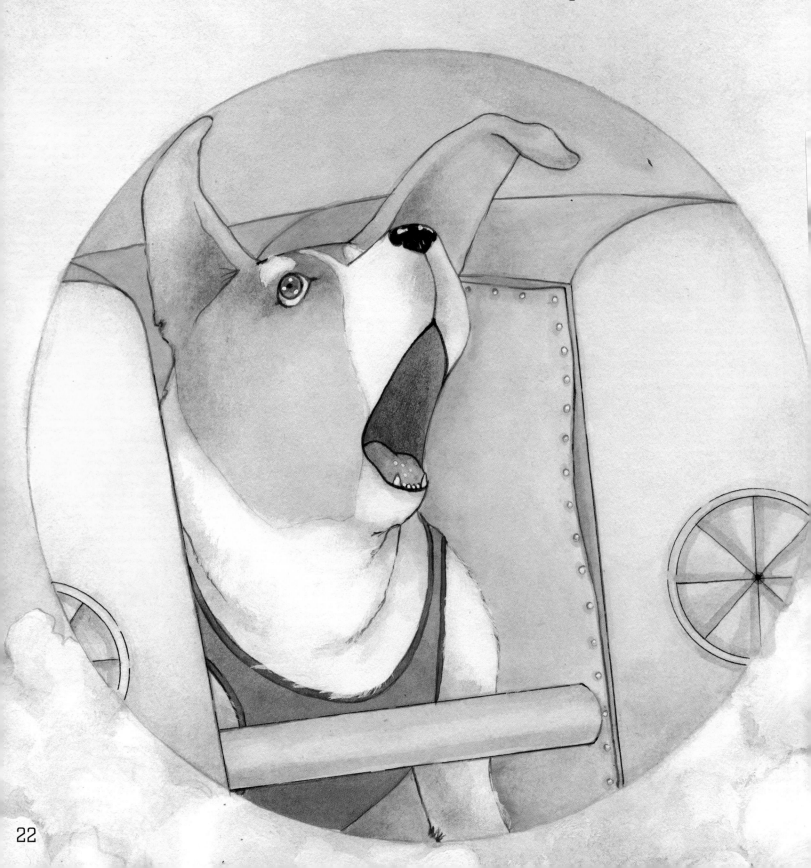

A small crowd watched as the gleaming Soviet spacecraft sped up through the sky and out of sight. People across the Soviet Union cheered for one brave pup, the world's first true astronaut.

Scientists received the reports *Sputnik 2* sent down to Earth. Laika's heart rate, blood pressure, and movements showed she had completed her mission. A little stray the world called "Laika" whirled around the planet at 18,000 miles (28,968 kilometers) per hour.

A few hours into her flight, the cabin began to overheat. There
was nothing Laika could do. Her body gave in to heat and fright.
For Laika, the trip had ended.

But this tiny hero paved the way for many human astronauts to come.

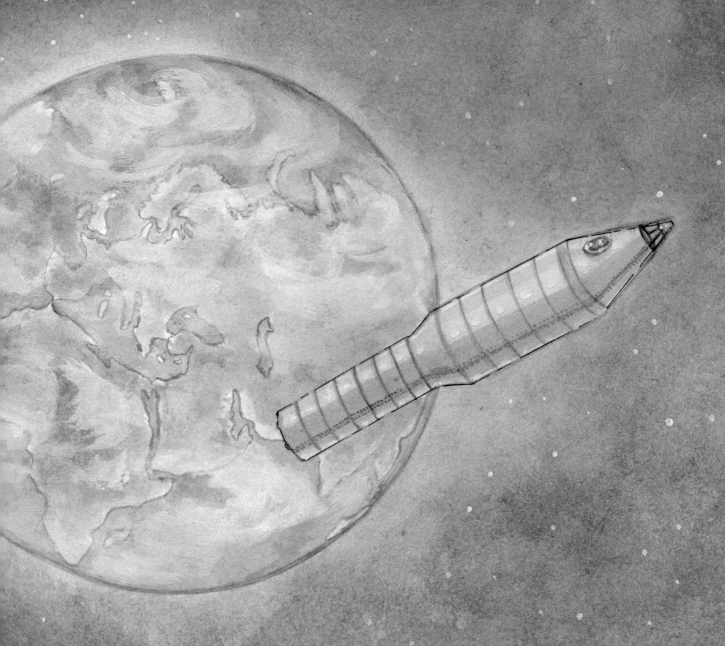

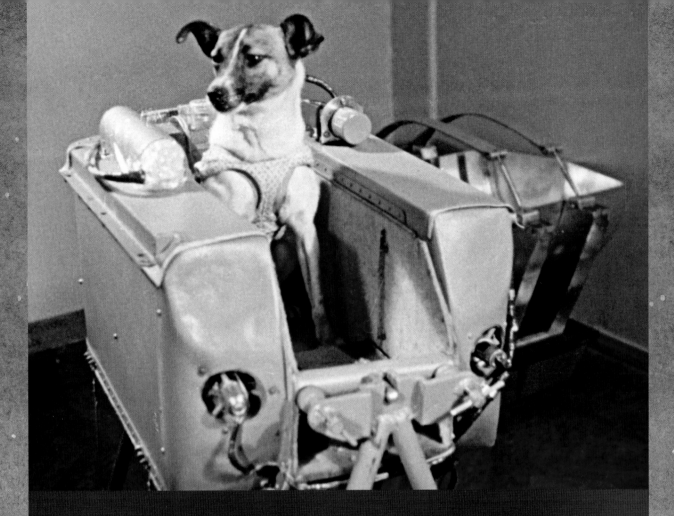

AFTERWORD

After Laika's death, *Sputnik 2* continued to orbit Earth for many months. Finally, on April 14, 1958, *Sputnik 2* reentered Earth's atmosphere. Catching fire, it fell back toward the earth. The satellite burned up before ever reaching land.

Thanks to Laika and many other animal heroes, space travel became a reality for humans less than five years later. In 1961, Russian Yuri Gagarin became the first person to launch into outer space. Oleg Gazenko, Laika's trainer, was one of the people who helped Gagarin prepare for his launch.

Laika was the only creature sent to outer space without a plan to safely return.

In 2007, exactly 50 years after her launch, a statue of Laika was unveiled in Moscow to honor her courage and sacrifice.

GLOSSARY

LABORATORY—a place where scientists do experiments and tests

LAUNCH—to send a rocket or spacecraft into space

LAUNCHPAD—a large area where a spacecraft is loaded and blasts off into space

ORBIT—to travel around an object in space; an orbit is also the path an object follows while circling an object in space.

SATELLITE—an object that moves around a planet or other cosmic body

READ MORE

Dunn, Joeming W. *Laika: the 1st Dog in Space.* Animals Making History. Edina, Minn.: Magic Wagon, 2012.

Hoena, Blake. *Stubby the Dog Soldier: World War I Hero.* Animal Heroes. North Mankato, Minn.: Picture Window Books, 2015.

Jefferis, David. *Race into Space.* New York: Crabtree Pub., 2007.